NTSB/PAR-14/01
PB2014-103977
Notation 8545
Adopted February 19, 2014

Pipeline Accident Report

Columbia Gas Transmission Corporation Pipeline Rupture
Sissonville, West Virginia
December 11, 2012

**National
Transportation
Safety Board**

490 L'Enfant Plaza, SW
Washington, DC 20594

National Transportation Safety Board. 2014. *Columbia Gas Transmission Corporation Pipeline Rupture, Sissonville, West Virginia, December 11, 2012*. Pipeline Accident Report. NTSB/PAR-14/01. Washington, DC.

Abstract: On December 11, 2012, at 12:41 p.m. eastern standard time, a buried 20-inch-diameter interstate natural gas transmission pipeline, owned and operated by Columbia Gas Transmission Corporation, ruptured in a sparsely populated area, about 106 feet west of Interstate 77 near Route 21 and Derricks Creek Road, in Sissonville, West Virginia. About 20 feet of pipe was separated and ejected from the underground pipeline and landed more than 40 feet from its original location. The escaping high-pressure natural gas ignited immediately. An area of fire damage about 820 feet wide extended nearly 1,100 feet along the pipeline right-of-way. Three houses were destroyed by the fire, and several other houses were damaged. There were no fatalities or serious injuries. About 76 million standard cubic feet of natural gas was released and burned. Columbia Gas Transmission Corporation reported the cost of pipeline repair was $2.9 million, the cost of system upgrades to accommodate in-line inspection was $5.5 million, and the cost of gas loss was $285,000.

Major safety issues identified in this investigation were external corrosion mitigation of the ruptured pipeline, supervisory control and data acquisition alert setpoint configuration, use of automatic shutoff valves and remote control valves to improve isolation of high-pressure pipelines, and exclusion of pipelines in the vicinity of highways from integrity management regulation. The National Transportation Safety Board makes safety recommendations to Columbia Gas Transmission Corporation and the Pipeline and Hazardous Materials Safety Administration.

Contents

Figures

Tables

Abbreviations and Acronyms

ANSI   American National Standards Institute

API   American Petroleum Institute

ASME   American Society of Mechanical Engineers

ASV   automatic shutoff valve

Cabot   Cabot Oil & Gas Corporation

CAO   corrective action order

CFR   *Code of Federal Regulations*

CIS   close interval survey

Clendenin   Clendenin compressor station

Columbia Gas Columbia Gas Transmission Corporation

ERW   electric resistance weld

HCA   high consequence area

I-77   Interstate 77

ILI   in-line inspection

IM   integrity management

ISA   International Society of Automation

Lanham   Lanham compressor station

MAOP   maximum allowable operating pressure

Metro 911   Metro Emergency Operations Center

PG&E   Pacific Gas and Electric Company

PHMSA   Pipeline and Hazardous Materials Safety Administration

PIR   potential impact radius

PSC   Public Service Commission of West Virginia

psi   pounds per square inch

psig   pounds per square inch, gauge

RCV   remote control valve

SCADA   supervisory control and data acquisition

Executive Summary

On December 11, 2012, at 12:41 p.m. eastern standard time, a buried 20-inch-diameter interstate natural gas transmission pipeline (Line SM-80), owned and operated by Columbia Gas Transmission Corporation, ruptured in a sparsely populated area, about 106 feet west of Interstate 77 near Route 21 and Derricks Creek Road, in Sissonville, West Virginia. About 20 feet of pipe was separated and ejected from the underground pipeline and landed more than 40 feet from its original location. According to Columbia Gas Transmission Corporation, the maximum allowable operating pressure of the pipeline was 1,000 pounds per square inch, gauge, and the operating pressure at the time of the rupture was about 929 pounds per square inch, gauge.

The ruptured pipe was part of a pipeline segment that was installed in 1967 and was in a Class 2 location, indicating that an area 220 yards (200 meters) on either side of the centerline of the pipeline had between 10 and 46 buildings intended for human occupancy. According to Columbia Gas Transmission Corporation records, the 20-inch-diameter pipeline segment had a nominal wall thickness of 0.281 inch and a longitudinal electric resistance weld seam. Corrosion protection was provided by a factory-applied polymer coating and impressed current cathodic protection.

The ruptured pipe was oriented with the longitudinal seam weld near the top of the pipe. The fracture was located in the base metal at the bottom of the pipe along the longitudinal direction. The outside pipe surface was heavily corroded near the midpoint of the rupture and along the longitudinal fracture. The corroded area was about 6 feet long in the longitudinal direction and 2 feet wide in the circumferential direction. The smallest measured wall thickness was 0.078 inch (more than 70 percent wall loss).

The escaping high-pressure natural gas ignited. Fire damage extended nearly 1,100 feet along the pipeline right-of-way and covered an area about 820 feet wide. Three houses were destroyed by the fire, and several other houses were damaged. There were no fatalities or serious injuries; however, Interstate 77 was closed for 19 hours until about 800 feet of thermally damaged road surface was replaced.

The National Transportation Safety Board determines that the probable cause of the pipeline rupture was (1) external corrosion of the pipe wall due to deteriorated coating and ineffective cathodic protection and (2) the failure to detect the corrosion because the pipeline was not inspected or tested after 1988. Contributing to the poor condition of the corrosion protection systems was the rocky backfill used around the buried pipe. Contributing to the delay in the controller's recognition of the rupture was Columbia Gas Transmission Corporation management's inadequate configuration of the alerts in the supervisory control and data acquisition system. Contributing to the delay in isolating the rupture was the lack of automatic shutoff or remote control valves.

This report discusses the following safety issues:

- External corrosion mitigation of pipeline SM-80

- Supervisory control and data acquisition alert setpoint configuration

- Use of automatic shutoff valves and remote control valves to improve isolation of high-pressure pipelines

- Exclusion of pipelines in the vicinity of highways from integrity management regulation

1. Investigation and Analysis

1.1 Accident Narrative

On December 11, 2012, at 12:41 p.m. eastern standard time,[1] a buried 20-inch-diameter interstate natural gas transmission pipeline (Line SM-80), owned and operated by Columbia Gas Transmission Corporation (Columbia Gas), ruptured in a sparsely populated area, about 106 feet west of Interstate 77 (I-77) near Route 21 and Derricks Creek Road in Sissonville in Kanawha County, West Virginia. The pipeline was operating at about 929 pounds per square inch, gauge (psig), just before the rupture. About 20 feet of pipe was ejected from the underground pipeline and landed more than 40 feet away. (See figure 1.)

Figure 1. Accident scene facing east.

Two other Columbia Gas transmission lines—a 26-inch-diameter pipeline (Line SM-86) and a 30-inch-diameter pipeline (Line SM-86 Loop)—located within the same right-of-way as Line SM-80 were not damaged. (See figure 2.)

---

[1] Unless otherwise specified, all times in this report are eastern standard time.

Figure 2. Aerial view of the routes of the three SM-80 system pipelines and the rupture location.

The ruptured pipe was part of a pipeline segment that was installed and pressure-tested in 1967 and was in a Class 2 location.[2] The failed pipe joint was 37 feet 8 1/2 inches long.[3] (See figure 3.) It had a nominal wall thickness of 0.281 inch and a longitudinal electric resistance weld (ERW) seam oriented at the top of the pipe. It was manufactured by American Steel according to the American Petroleum Institute (API) Standard 5L grade X60. Corrosion protection was provided by a factory-applied polymer coating, a field-applied coal tar, and impressed current cathodic protection.[4]

---

[2] Regulations for gas transmission pipelines establish pipe strength requirements based on population density near the pipeline. Locations along gas pipelines are divided into classes from 1 (rural) to 4 (densely populated) and are based upon the number of buildings or dwellings for human occupancy. The safety margin of the pipeline, or ratio of the design pressure to the maximum allowable operating pressure, is greatest in a Class 4 location.

[3] A pipe joint is defined as the length of pipe between two adjacent girth (circumferential) welds.

[4] Cathodic protection is a corrosion mitigation method used by the pipeline industry to protect underground steel structures. The system uses direct current power supplies at selected locations along the pipeline to supply protective electrical current. The impressed current is supplied to the pipeline through a ground bed that typically contains a string of anodes, with soil as the electrolyte. A wire connected to the pipeline provides the return path for the current to complete the circuit.

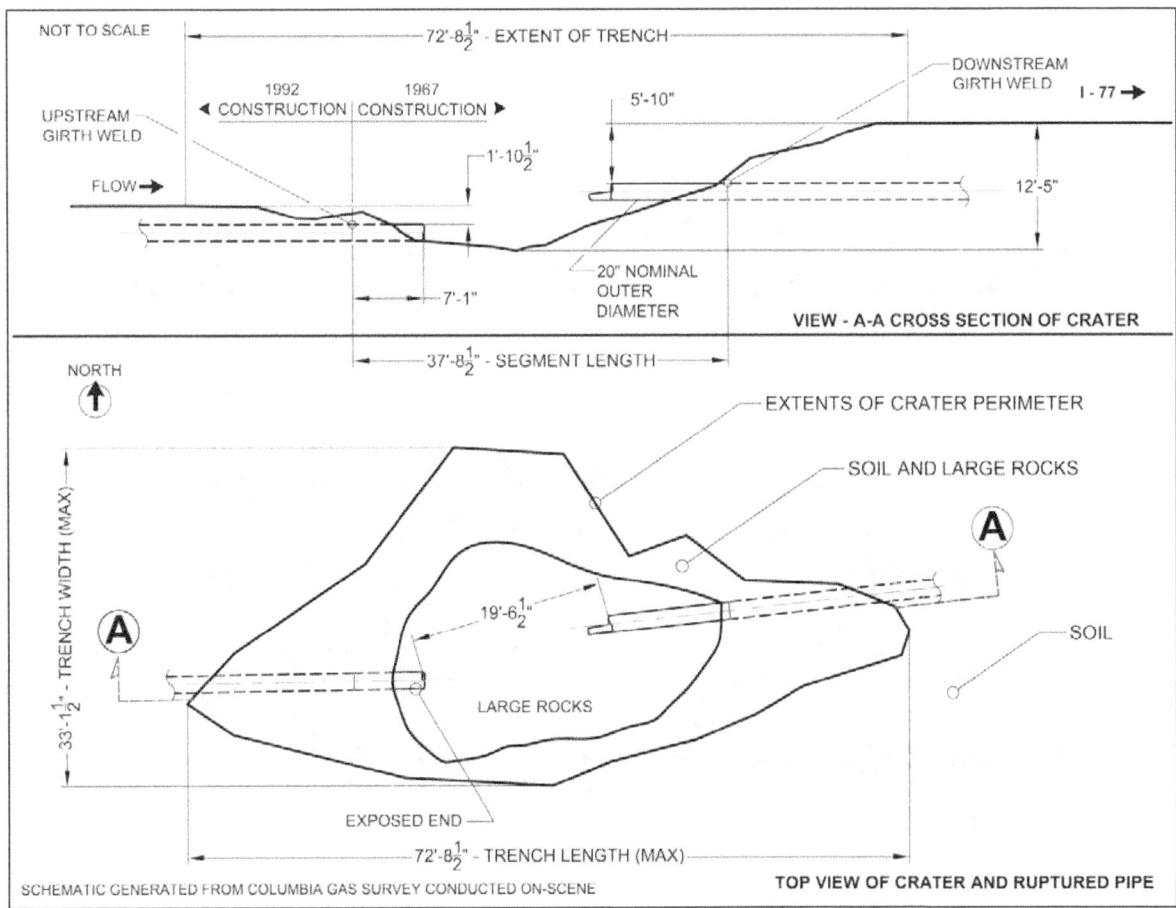

Figure 3. Line SM-80 schematic showing pipeline rupture detail.

The 20-foot-long ejected pipe contained no girth welds. The rupture initiated in an area of heavy external corrosion along the bottom of the pipe that measured about 6 feet in the longitudinal direction and 2 feet in the circumferential direction. The smallest measured wall thickness near the initiation site was 0.078 inch (more than 70 percent wall loss). The pipe fractured in the longitudinal direction along the entire 20-foot length.

The escaping high-pressure natural gas ignited immediately. An area of fire damage about 820 feet wide extended nearly 1,100 feet along the pipeline right-of-way. Three houses were destroyed by the fire, and several other houses were damaged. There were no fatalities or serious injuries. The asphalt pavement of the northbound and southbound lanes of I-77 was heavily damaged by the intense fire. Work crews repaired and reopened all four lanes of the highway about 18 hours later. About 76 million standard cubic feet of natural gas was released and burned. Columbia Gas reported the cost of pipeline repair was $2.9 million, the cost of system upgrades to accommodate in-line inspection (ILI) was $5.5 million, and the cost of gas loss was $285,000.

The first call to 911 was made by a person at a nearby retirement home at 12:41 p.m. The Columbia Gas control center received a verbal notification of the rupture about 12:53 p.m. from a Cabot Oil & Gas Corporation (Cabot) controller who had received a report of a rupture and fire from a field technician near the accident location. Cabot operates other pipelines in the region and supplies natural gas to Columbia Gas.

1.2 Columbia Gas Transmission Corporation

Columbia Gas is owned by Columbia Pipeline Group, a NiSource company.[5] Columbia Gas transports an average of 3 billion cubic feet of natural gas per day through a nearly 12,000-mile pipeline network with 92 compressor stations in 10 states. The SM-80 pipeline system consists of three interconnected pipelines transporting unodorized natural gas: Line SM-80, a 20-inch-diameter line; Line SM-86, a 26-inch-diameter line; and Line SM-86 Loop, a 30-inch-diameter line. The SM-80 system is part of a larger pipeline network operated by Columbia Gas called the Charleston system.

Corrosion of these three pipelines is mitigated by external coating and impressed current cathodic protection. All three lines shared the same right-of-way near the accident site, had the same 1,000 psig maximum allowable operating pressure (MAOP), and were cross-connected upstream and downstream of the rupture location. Line SM-86 was about 165 feet away from the rupture location on Line SM-80, and Line SM-86 Loop was about 40 feet away from the rupture location.

1.2.1 Line SM-80

Line SM-80 originates at Lanham compressor station (Lanham) near Sissonville, West Virginia. It is 29.6 miles long and terminates upstream of the Broad Run valve station near Clendenin, West Virginia. The SM-80 pipeline was installed in the early 1950s as an uncoated steel pipeline.

Pipeline records indicate that during the construction of I-77 in 1967, a 717-foot segment of the original pipeline was replaced with a 20-inch-diameter, 0.281-inch-thick API Standard 5L grade X60 pipe segment with fusion-bonded epoxy coating and a field-applied coal tar enamel. After the rupture, the excavated pipe was found to be coated with a green material, which laboratory testing identified as a polymer. Line SM-80 was pressure-tested twice in 1967, once at the time of the replacement project and again during a hydrostatic test of the entire 29.6-mile span. Both tests were performed for 8 hours, and the highest test pressure was 1,800 psig.

In 1992, Columbia Gas replaced segments of Line SM-80 upstream and downstream of the 1967 replacement pipe with new, 20-inch-diameter API Standard 5L grade X60 ERW pipe manufactured by American Steel. The wall thickness of the upstream segment was 0.281 inch, and of the downstream segment, 0.25 inch. Both new segments had a mill-applied coal tar enamel coating. Following the 1992 replacement project, 654 feet of the 1967 pipe remained in Line SM-80 at the crossing near I-77, where the rupture occurred. According to Columbia Gas, no corrosion-related leaks had occurred in the SM-80 system before the December 11, 2012, rupture.

---

[5] At the time of the accident, Columbia Gas was owned by NiSource Gas Transmission and Storage.

The area where Line SM-80 ruptured is rural and sparsely populated, and Line SM-80 in that area was designated as being in a Class 2 location. The ruptured pipe was not within a high consequence area (HCA).[6] Therefore, Line SM-80 was not covered by the requirements in Title 49 *Code of Federal Regulations* (CFR) Part 192, Subpart O, *Gas Transmission Pipeline Integrity Management*. Accordingly, Line SM-80 was not part of the Columbia Gas integrity management (IM) program.

In addition to discharge isolation valves at Lanham, Line SM-80 was outfitted with mainline isolation valves at the Rocky Hollow and Patterson Fork valve stations. The Rocky Hollow valves were 7.9 miles downstream from Lanham, and the Patterson Fork valves were 15.6 miles downstream from Lanham. (See figure 4.)

1.2.2 Line SM-86 Loop

Line SM-86 Loop is primarily a 30-inch-diameter API Standard 5L grade X65 0.321-inch-thick natural gas pipeline with coal tar coating. It runs from the Lanham compressor station to the Panther Mountain valve station near Clendenin, West Virginia. The pipeline is about 26.6 miles long. According to Columbia Gas, and based on the 1,000 psig MAOP and the pipe diameter, a 353-foot-long segment of this pipeline adjacent to the rupture location was designated to be in an HCA Class 2 location.

1.2.3 Line SM-86

Line SM-86 is a 26-inch-diameter natural gas pipeline that runs from Lanham Compressor Station to the Panther Mountain valve station. The pipeline is 26.5 miles long and shares the right-of-way with Line SM-86 Loop for nearly its entire length. According to Columbia Gas, and based on the 1,000 psig MAOP and pipe diameter, a 303-foot-long segment of this pipeline adjacent to the rupture location was designated to be in an HCA Class 1 location.

---

[6] An HCA is determined along each pipeline based on the population density within the potential impact radius (PIR), which is a function of the pipe diameter and the MAOP. (See 49 CFR 192.5 and 192.903.) The population density in the Line SM-80 PIR was below the threshold value for an HCA. Each pipeline HCA is independent of any pipeline that passes through it and any overlapping HCA from an adjacent pipeline. The HCA determination is also independent of the pipeline class determination.

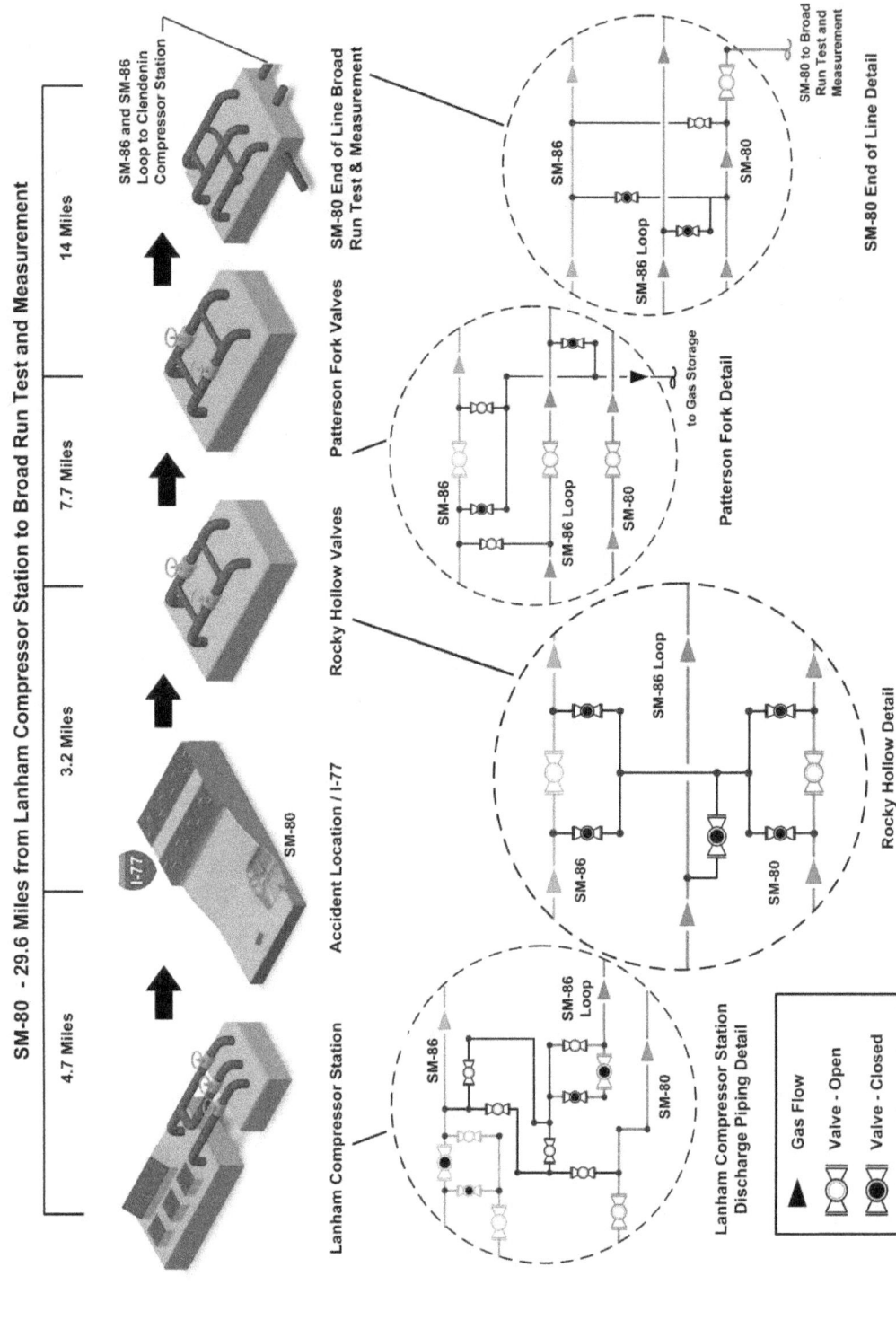

Figure 4. Line SM-80 system schematic showing isolation valve locations and positions at time of rupture.

1.2.4 Automatic Shutoff Valves and Remote Control Valves

When a high-pressure gas transmission pipeline ruptures, structures near the epicenter typically sustain sudden catastrophic damage. The extent of the damage to structures farther away from the epicenter and the intense gas-fueled fire is proportional to the time required to isolate the gas supply and extinguish the fires on both sides of the rupture. Automatic shutoff valves (ASVs) and remote control valves (RCVs) can significantly shorten the rupture isolation time because they quickly and automatically close when the pipeline pressure drops to a preset value. The valve closing response time is not dependent on the controllers' recognizing a rupture or on the time it takes for pipeline mechanics to be notified, travel to the valve sites, and close the valves.

Pipeline operators are required by 49 CFR 192.935 to use a risk analysis method to determine if and where ASVs and RCVs are needed on pipelines containing HCAs. Columbia Gas uses a three-step process to determine if ASVs or RCVs are needed in a pipeline HCA and if so, the type of valves to use and where they are installed.[7] Although Line SM-86 and Line SM-86 Loop contained HCAs, the risk analysis did not identify the need to install ASVs or RCVs on either pipeline. Because Line SM-80 was not in an HCA, it was not evaluated, so it did not contain either ASVs or RCVs. All the isolation valves on the three pipeline systems were locally operated; some were fitted with motor operators, and the other valves were operated manually.

When the pipeline ruptured, more than 1 hour passed before field personnel completed closing all the SM-80 system valves, which isolated the rupture location from the gas supply. Automatic shutoff valves would most likely have shortened that time. The National Transportation Safety Board (NTSB) first examined how ASVs and RCVs can shorten the duration of the intense gas-fueled fire at a pipeline rupture site in a pipeline accident in Edison, New Jersey, in 1994 (NTSB 1995). Currently, the regulations do not specify a length of time to isolate a ruptured gas line, other than for pipelines with an alternative MAOP.[8] Furthermore, the regulations give the pipeline operator discretion to decide whether ASVs or RCVs are needed in HCAs as long as the pipeline operator considers the factors listed under 49 CFR 192.935(c).[9]

The NTSB revisited the ASV/RCV issue in the investigation of the September 9, 2010, Pacific Gas and Electric Company (PG&E) natural gas transmission pipeline rupture in San Bruno, California, in which eight people died, 38 houses were destroyed, and 70 houses were damaged (NTSB 2011). As a result of the accident, the NTSB issued the following recommendation to the Pipeline and Hazardous Materials Safety Administration (PHMSA):

---

[7] An ASV closes automatically based on predetermined pressure and flow setpoints. An RCV is operated by a controller in the control center. Both types of valves eliminate the need for a technician to travel to the valve location to open or close the valve, which can significantly shorten the time required to isolate a pipe segment.

[8] Title 49 CFR 192.620, *Alternative Maximum Allowable Operating Pressure for Certain Steel Pipelines*, allows a pipeline operator to operate a pipeline at up to 80 percent specified minimum yield strength in Class 2 locations as long as the pipeline operator meets a very specific and stringent set of criteria listed in the regulation.

[9] The decision factors for using an ASV or an RCV in a pipeline are (1) the swiftness of leak detection and pipe shutoff capabilities, (2) the type of gas being transported, (3) the operating pressure, (4) the gas flow rate of potential release, (5) the pipeline profile, (6) the potential for ignition, and (7) the location of the nearest response personnel.

<u>P-11-11</u>

Amend Title 49 *Code of Federal Regulations* 192.935(c) to directly require that automatic shutoff valves or remote control valves in high consequence areas and in class 3 and 4 locations be installed and spaced at intervals that consider the factors listed in that regulation. (Classified "Open—Acceptable Response" on April 24, 2012)

1.2.5 Control Center

The Columbia Gas pipeline system is monitored and controlled from a single supervisory control and data acquisition (SCADA) system in the Columbia Gas control center in Charleston, West Virginia. The control center is staffed with three to five gas controllers who operate specific pipeline systems from five consoles. The day shift works from 6:00 a.m. to 6:00 p.m., and the night shift works from 6:00 p.m. to 6:00 a.m. Each controller is assigned not more than two pipelines. Each pipeline can be controlled using the SCADA system at any of the consoles. The controller is responsible for monitoring the SCADA system, using various SCADA indications, alerts, and alarms to identify pipeline leaks.[10]

On the day of the accident, the Charleston and Commonwealth pipeline systems were monitored by one controller.[11] The SM-80 system is part of the Charleston system. Other controllers and supervisors (the manager and the director of gas control) also were present and monitoring control room operations at the time of the accident.

Columbia Gas upgraded its SCADA system in 2011 and reconfigured and consolidated the display screens using the guidance referenced in the PHMSA control room management rule issued November 20, 2009, and codified at 49 CFR 192.631. To reduce the frequency of nuisance alarms, Columbia Gas configured the SCADA system with two event categories: alarms and alerts. Each controller has one dedicated display monitor at the console that lists alarms and alerts. The listing is divided into three areas, or grids. The alarms and alerts are displayed on different grids. The most recent alarm or alert is displayed on the top line of its grid and flashes until it is acknowledged.

The limiting value, or setpoint, for each process parameter can be designated as an alarm or alert. For example, a regulator discharge pressure may have a high alarm limit. The same discharge pressure may have an alert value set for a specified pressure change. The controller must acknowledge every alarm and alert individually.[12]

Columbia Gas defines the term *alarm* as "an audible or visible means of indicating to the controller that equipment or processes are outside of [pipeline] operator-defined, safety-related

---

[10] The SM-80 system does not have an automated leak-detection system.

[11] Columbia Gas assigns names to the pipeline systems for convenience: Charleston, for example. Each system contains multiple smaller systems: for example, SM-80.

[12] A controller acknowledges alarms and alerts by a keyboard entry or clicking with a mouse on the SCADA system display screen.

parameters," which is consistent with the federal regulation (NiSource 2012). Columbia Gas defines the term *safety related* as "any operational factor that is necessary to maintain pipeline integrity or that could lead to the recognition of a condition that could impact the integrity of the pipeline, or a developing abnormal emergency situation" (NiSource 2012). Alarms display in red and require the controller to take immediate action to correct the situation, including shutting down the affected pipeline segment.

Columbia Gas defines the term *alert* as follows:

an audible or visible means of indicating to the controller or monitoring center analyst that conditions have changed, equipment or other monitoring variables are outside of operator defined controlling parameters or which indicate that equipment, devices or processes are not functioning as intended but which are not integral to a safety-related parameter. (NiSource 2012)

A control system alert has no regulatory definition. The process variable and setpoint for each alert can be assigned by the controller, and different controllers can select different alerts for the same pipeline segment. The SCADA system default value for alert setpoints is 5 percent or 5 units of the process variable. Columbia Gas provides no guidance for alert parameter selection. Furthermore, Columbia Gas did not provide guidance on how and when alerts can provide useful information to the controller.

Alerts are displayed in green or yellow based on the controller-assigned level of importance; yellow is the more important indicator. Alerts are intended to assist the controller in monitoring and controlling the pipeline system during normal demand changes. Columbia Gas relies on the controller to recognize an abnormal condition from the SCADA system alerts or other indications. However, management did not provide any guidance or instructions to the controllers related to alert parameter settings or appropriate action for alerts. At the time of the accident, pressure deviation alerts for the SM-80 system were set to activate if a pressure value at the Lanham discharge valves on any of the three lines increased or decreased by at least 10 psig (1 percent of the MAOP). The low-low pressure alarm setpoint for the compressor discharge pressure for the SM-80 system was 500 psig.

According to Columbia Gas operating records for the 19-month period ending February 28, 2013, the Charleston and Commonwealth pipeline systems had a combined average of 1.9 alarms per hour. This alarm frequency was within the industry guideline for control room design. SCADA guidelines do not provide any recommendations for maximum displayed alert frequency. Although Columbia Gas SCADA records indicated that an average of 83 alerts per hour occurred on the two pipeline systems, the controller told NTSB investigators that typical alert notifications during his duty time "did not overwhelm" him.

1.3 Preaccident Events

1.3.1 Line SM-80

No requests to locate buried utilities in the vicinity of the rupture were made to Columbia Gas in the 3 months preceding the rupture. No excavation activity was evident at or near the rupture location during the NTSB field investigation. Therefore, the NTSB concludes that third-party direct pipeline impact damage was not a factor in this accident.

Line SM-80 was operating at 929 psig (discharge pressure at Lanham) when the rupture occurred. The SCADA system records confirm that there were no significant valve position changes, pressure transients, or other abnormal conditions before the rupture.

1.3.2 Columbia Gas Controller

On the day of the accident a Columbia Gas controller with 20 years of experience was operating the SCADA system for the Charleston and the Commonwealth pipeline systems, a function he routinely performed. He was qualified to operate pipelines on multiple territories. He was responsible for all operations of the pipelines, including monitoring each SCADA system alarm and alert screen. He described his work on the morning of December 11, 2012, as routine and his workload as normal; he also described his work and workload on the days before the accident as being the same.

The controller told investigators that before reporting to work at 6:00 a.m., he had slept for about 8 hours the night before. His commute time to work was 10 minutes. He also stated that his overall health was good and that he had not taken any prescription or nonprescription medications before reporting to work. His postaccident toxicological test results were negative for illicit drugs and alcohol. Therefore, the NTSB concludes that the controller was experienced and qualified, fit for duty, not physically fatigued, and not under the influence of illicit drugs or alcohol on the day of the accident.

1.4 Response to Pipeline Rupture

1.4.1 Local Emergency Response

At 12:41 p.m., the Metro Emergency Operations Center (Metro 911) received the first 911 call.[13] The caller reported that a "gas main blew up" and there was a huge fire near Archibald Drive in Sissonville. At 12:43 p.m., firefighters from Sissonville Volunteer Fire Department Station 26 and Malden Fire Department Station 3 were paged to respond. Between 12:42 p.m. and 12:50 p.m., additional fire companies, emergency medical services, and Kanawha County sheriff deputies were dispatched to respond to the accident. An emergency medical services medic was the first to arrive on scene about 12:49 p.m.

---

[13] The Metro Emergency Operations Center is the emergency services dispatch center for Kanawha County, West Virginia.

A Sissonville fire department lieutenant and a firefighter responded to the accident scene with a fire engine, and upon arrival at the scene, the lieutenant assumed incident command. The Sissonville fire chief responded to the accident scene with a tanker, and while en route, he began communicating with the other responders to ensure that enough fire department and law enforcement resources were dispatched. On his arrival at the scene, he assumed incident command and requested that the dispatch center notify the gas companies operating in the accident area.

The incident command post was established on Route 21. Police closed Route 21 and I-77 and set up a security perimeter around the accident site. Additional fire engines and tankers were requested and obtained from surrounding fire departments. As responders continued arriving on scene, they reported to Metro 911 that there was heavy smoke and fire in the area and it appeared to be a natural gas fire. Metro 911 began notifying gas companies operating in the area at 1:01 p.m. At 1:06 p.m., Metro 911 notified Appalachian Power of the incident to ensure power was shut down at the accident location. At 1:15 p.m., Metro 911 spoke with personnel at the Columbia Gas Lanham compressor station and asked them to shut down "the main line that was on fire."

Metro 911 notified the incident commander that a woman was trapped in her house on Route 21, so a fire engine company entered the house and rescued her. After the flow of gas was stopped, firefighters worked to suppress the house fires near the rupture. However, three houses and some vehicles parked nearby were destroyed. The incident commander concluded fire operations about 10:00 p.m.

1.4.2 Response of Cabot and Columbia Gas Control Centers

The NTSB investigators examined the SCADA operating records for the day of the accident. Pressure recordings for the Lanham pump station discharge pressures show that at 12:41 p.m. the Line SM-80 discharge pressure began to drop. (See figure 5.) About 12:42 p.m., a Cabot compressor operator who was driving near the accident site called the Cabot control center to report that he had just heard a huge "boom" that "sounded like a bomb going off" and asked whether the control center had received reports of or observed any SCADA system indications that might indicate a problem on the Cabot pipeline system. The Cabot controller told him that the system parameters were normal.

Four minutes later, the Cabot compressor operator called the Cabot controller again and reported that he now was observing "big flames shooting over the interstate." The controller told investigators that during his phone conversation with the compressor operator, "I was just looking at my screen and I'm not seeing anything happening." The Cabot controller and his manager decided to call the Columbia Gas control center and tell them about the fire, because both companies have pipelines in the vicinity of the reported fire.[14]

---

[14] Cabot is a customer of Columbia Gas and has a bidirectional 8-inch-diameter interconnect (storage line) at the Columbia Gas Lanham compressor station.

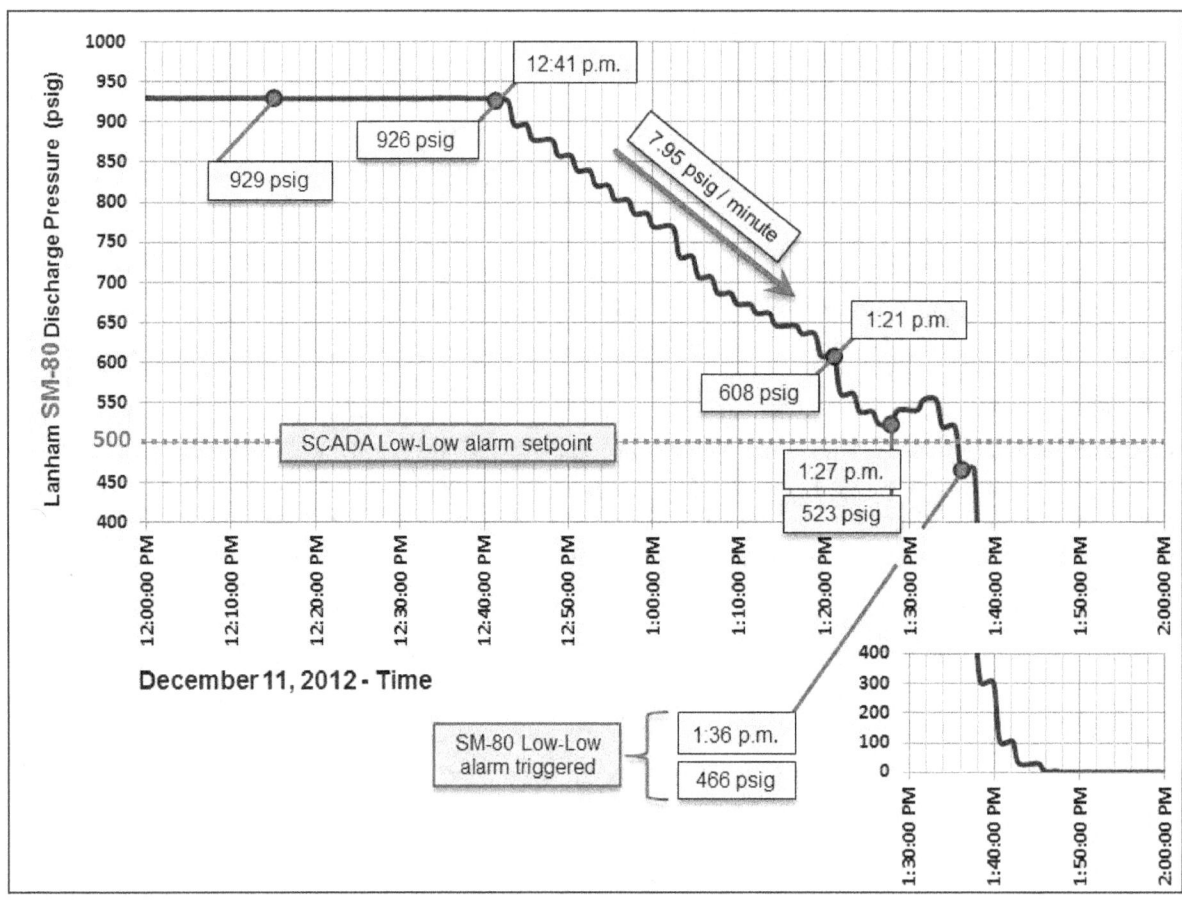

Figure 5. Line SM-80 discharge pressure at Lanham compressor station just before and after the rupture.

About 12:53 p.m., the Cabot controller called the Columbia Gas control center and talked to the on-duty controller responsible for the SM-80 system. The Cabot controller explained that he had a report of fire at Derricks Creek and Route 21, and he asked the Columbia Gas controller whether he was having any problems on the Columbia Gas pipeline or seeing any pressure drops. The Cabot controller told investigators that "at the time I don't think [the Columbia Gas controller] really knew [whether there was a problem] just by the way he acted. He kind of acted like he was searching to see [whether there was a problem]." The Columbia Gas controller examined the system displays and responded that he was seeing some pressure drops on the Charleston system. At that point, they agreed that the problem was on the Columbia Gas pipeline. As a precaution, the Cabot controller closed the remote control isolation valves between the Cabot system and the Lanham compressor station to isolate the Cabot pipeline system from the Columbia Gas system.

At 12:55 p.m., as the Columbia Gas controller ended the call with Cabot, the sixth alert displayed on the SCADA system console. The controller told investigators he then walked to the office of the director of gas control and informed him of a possible leak in the SM-80 system. Although the Columbia Gas operations staff at that point recognized the problem most likely was in their system, the operating data displayed on the SCADA system were insufficient for the

Columbia Gas controller to identify which of the three interconnected pipelines in the SM-80 system had ruptured.

The NTSB reviewed the SCADA data records for the accident date. The first indication of a problem on the Charleston pipeline system was at 12:43 p.m. when three discharge pressure deviation alerts at the Lanham compressor station were simultaneously presented on the SCADA system alert screen. The alerts were set to trigger when the pressure changed by more than 10 psig (1 percent of the MAOP). The SCADA logs showed two more sets of three compressor discharge pressure deviation alerts at 12:45 p.m. and 12:48 p.m. These three-alert groupings occurred because the isolation valves on the interconnects between the three SM-80 system pipelines were open and the pressure transducers on each pipeline were in the same relative position downstream of the compressor.

The next SCADA pressure deviation alert occurred on Line SM-80 at 12:49 p.m., 25 miles downstream of the rupture at the Broad Run valve station, indicating a 50-psig pressure change. The controller next received and acknowledged two more groups of three Lanham pump station discharge pressure deviation alerts, at 12:50 p.m. and 12:52 p.m. Based on the SCADA system information for the Lanham compressor station discharge pressure trends and pressure creep alerts, the NTSB concludes that Line SM-80 ruptured at 12:41 p.m.

The SCADA alert screen displayed the parameter and its indicated value, but it did not indicate whether the new value was an increase or decrease or display the amount of the change. To understand the significance of the alert, the controller had to know the value of the previous parameter, either from the prior displayed alert value or from observing the parameter on a system display screen. Recognizing the significance of alerts was further complicated by the fact that the controller was reviewing and responding to other SCADA parameters on the two pipeline systems he was overseeing during the 1- to 2-minute spans between the pressure deviation alerts.

Although the controller acknowledged each deviation alert at the compressor discharge 5 miles upstream of the rupture, he did not examine the system parameters to clearly understand that the pressure on all three lines was continuing to drop. Furthermore, even though before receiving the call from the Cabot control center the controller had received the 50-psig deviation alert at Broad Run, he still did not recognize the significance of the alerts. The NTSB concludes that despite the many pressure deviation alerts occurring on the system over more than 12 minutes, the Columbia Gas controller did not recognize the significance of the situation or begin to shut down the system until after the Cabot controller called him. The NTSB recommends that Columbia Gas implement a process for selecting alert setpoints, and provide guidance to pipeline controllers on the expected alert response time, ways to evaluate the significance of alerts, and actions the controller must take in response to those alerts.

The NTSB concludes that the Columbia Gas SCADA system alerts did not provide useful, meaningful information to the controller to assist him in determining the operating condition of the pipeline. Therefore, the NTSB recommends that Columbia Gas modify its SCADA system to (1) provide the controller with operating parameter trend data that can be used to evaluate the significance of a system change and (2) assign an alarm function to trends that are likely significant system malfunctions and therefore require immediate action by the controller.

When the Columbia Gas controller and the Columbia director of gas control realized the SM-80 system was likely involved in the fire, the controller called the Lanham compressor station. The controller instructed the station operator to shut down the compressor immediately.[15] The SCADA system logs confirm that the compressor was stopped at 1:02 p.m.

Although the rupture severed Line SM-80, venting the large volume of natural gas contained in the three interconnected pipelines took 45 minutes before the system pressure decayed below the 500-psig low-low pressure alarm setpoint. This slow, prolonged pressure decay is typical in interconnected high-pressure natural gas pipelines and contributed to the damage caused by the burning gas. According to Columbia Gas, by 3:30 p.m., nearly 3 hours after the pipe ruptured, the gas-fueled fire had subsided, and the firefighters were able to enter and extinguish the structure fires. The NTSB concludes that strategically placed ASVs or RCVs would have isolated the three pipelines and shortened the duration of the intense fire.

1.4.3 Columbia Gas Emergency Response

About the same time the Columbia Gas controller was talking to the Cabot controller, a Columbia Gas corrosion specialist heard a radio news report of a 200-foot fireball in Sissonville while he was driving to a Columbia Gas field office in Ripley, West Virginia. He called a corrosion technician at 12:53 p.m. and asked the technician to send an emergency text message to the Columbia Gas East Operations manager, alerting him of the reported fire.

The East Operations manager was in transit about 21 miles from the accident site. The East Operations manager told investigators that as he was reading the emergency text, he received a phone call from the corrosion specialist, who told him, "I think we've got a failure at I-77 crossing." The East Operations manager began driving toward the accident site. The time was about 12:56 p.m. The technician also told him that several personnel at the Lanham compressor station were en route to close all the compressor station discharge valves to the SM-80 system.[16]

At 1:09 p.m., the East Operations manager called the Lanham mechanic and told him to close everything on the discharge side of the station and to notify him once all the valves were closed. He said to close all the valves because they did not yet know which of the three lines had ruptured. The Lanham isolation valves included four power-operated valves and two manual valves. The mechanics told NTSB investigators that it took about 15 minutes to close all six valves.[17]

---

[15] Compressor station personnel could shut down the compressor faster than the controller could remotely shut it down using the SCADA system in the control center.

[16] The discharge valves were located about 100 yards outside of the compressor facility, east of the main office of the Lanham compressor station.

[17] Because the three pipelines had multiple cross-connections at the valve stations, the controllers could not determine from the SCADA information screens exactly which of the three lines had ruptured. Therefore, they decided to close all the isolation valves at the Lanham and Patterson Fork valve stations to ensure that the rupture would be isolated from the gas supply as quickly as possible.

The East Operations manager then called the Clendenin Operations team leader and instructed him to send a crew to the Rocky Hollow and Patterson valve stations to close all of the SM-80 system isolation valves downstream of the rupture.

When the pipeline ruptured, two Columbia Gas operations personnel were repairing a leak on a production pipeline about 4.75 miles from the accident location and about 1.75 miles from the nearest downstream valves at the Rocky Hollow valve station. One of the operations personnel stated that they could hear the roar from the releasing gas. The men went to their truck and drove to a location where they could get cell phone connectivity.[18] One called the Columbia Gas control center and was told of the accident. They were familiar with the Lanham station and the pipelines in that area, so they drove to the nearest valve station at Rocky Hollow to close the valves and shut off the gas flow to Line SM-80. Columbia Gas estimated that the Rocky Hollow valves were shut by 1:32 p.m., which was confirmed by the SCADA system trends for Line SM-80 and Line SM-86.

After closing the discharge valves at the Lanham compressor station, the mechanics installed pressure gauges on the three lines to determine which pipeline had ruptured. Once all the isolation valves were closed at Rocky Hollow and Patterson Fork, the rupture was isolated from the gas supply. Gas pressure on Line SM-86 Loop stabilized at 575 psig and Line SM-86 stabilized between 475 psig and 500 psig. The pressure on Line SM-80 dropped to about zero psig, finally confirming that the rupture occurred on Line SM-80.

1.4.4 Surrounding Area Damage

Interstate 77 was closed in both directions because of the fire and road surface damage. The northbound lanes were closed for about 14 hours, and southbound lanes were closed for about 19 hours, while the road was resurfaced. The resurfaced area was about 800 feet long.

Thermal damage extended from the rupture point 490 feet to the north, 330 feet to the south, 470 feet to the east, and 610 feet to the west. Radiant heat and direct fire impingement destroyed three nearby houses and vehicles parked near the epicenter.

1.5 SCADA System Leak Detection

1.5.1 NTSB Accident Investigations

The NTSB has investigated other pipeline accidents involving pipeline controllers who did not detect, misinterpreted, or failed to appropriately respond to SCADA system alarms indicating an abnormal situation on the pipeline system. In many of these accidents, the NTSB identified shortcomings in the human-system interface.

---

[18] As a safety measure to minimize natural gas ignition sources, the workers had left their cellphones in the truck.

In the April 17, 1992, highly volatile liquid release from an underground storage cavern and explosion in Brenham, Texas, the NTSB noted that had the SCADA system provided a graphic display of historical operating data (which would have allowed the controller to see pressure and flow trends), the pipeline controller could have more easily recognized that the flow rate of highly volatile liquid into a storage cavern was abnormal. The NTSB concluded that the SCADA system did not display data from the storage station in a format that was easy for controllers to interpret, and issued the following safety recommendation to the American Gas Association and the API:

P-93-22

Develop standards and guidelines for the design and use of graphic information display systems used by dispatchers to control pipeline systems. (Classified Closed—Acceptable Action on June 5, 2007)

In the May 23, 1996, gasoline release near Gramercy, Louisiana, the pipeline controller misread an initial alarm for high pump-case pressure at a refinery that supplied product to the pipeline and attributed that alarm to normal activity at the refinery. He consequently attributed additional SCADA system alarms to similar activities without attending to the nature of each. Moreover, while reading the text of the line balance alarm, he did not notice that the line balance was negative, which indicated a potential leak. The NTSB determined that the controller's delay in recognizing the rupture delayed shutting down the pipeline and isolating the rupture and contributed to the severity of the accident (NTSB 1998). Damage exceeded $7.8 million. The NTSB made the following two safety recommendations to the pipeline operator, Marathon Ashland Pipe Line LLC:

P-98-21

Use recurrent pipeline controller training to (1) emphasize the importance of carefully and completely reading the text of and evaluating all alarm messages, and (2) increase controller proficiency in interpreting and responding to control system data that may indicate a system leak. (Classified Closed—Acceptable Action on April 28, 1999)

P-98-22

Evaluate the effectiveness of alternative display formats and frequencies of alarming critical information for your supervisory control and data acquisition system and modify the system as necessary to ensure that controllers are specifically prompted to consider the possibility of leaks during system deviations that are consistent with a loss of product from a pipeline. (Classified Closed—Acceptable Action on April 28, 1999)

In the November 5, 1996, diesel overpressure pipeline rupture in Murfreesboro, Tennessee, although the SCADA system registered a sudden 416-psig pressure drop when the line ruptured, no SCADA system alarms were generated. The NTSB determined that the probable cause of the accident, which caused $5.7 million in property damage, was

> (1) the failure of the pipeline [controller] to follow company procedures for operating the pipeline and (2) the failure of the [SCADA] system to inform the [controller] of unsafe conditions prior to the rupture. (NTSB 1999)

In the October 27, 2004, Kingman, Kansas, accident, the controller received numerous alarms within 5 minutes of the rupture. The controller erroneously determined that these alarms were caused by excessive delivery of ammonia from the pipeline and waited for the pressures to return to normal. The NTSB found that the controller did not use the available SCADA system trend screens to review and evaluate the alarms and abnormal conditions (NTSB 2007).

In its investigation of the September 9, 2010, rupture of the PG&E 30-inch-diameter intrastate natural gas transmission pipeline in San Bruno, California, the NTSB found that the PG&E SCADA system limitations contributed to the delay in recognizing that there had been a transmission line break and in quickly pinpointing its location (NTSB 2011). The NTSB consequently issued the following safety recommendation to PHMSA:

> P-11-10
>
> Require that all operators of natural gas transmission and distribution pipelines equip their supervisory control and data acquisition systems with tools to assist in recognizing and pinpointing the location of leaks, including line breaks; such tools could include a real-time leak detection system and appropriately spaced flow and pressure transmitters along covered transmission lines. (Classified Open—Acceptable Response on April 24, 2012)

1.5.2 NTSB SCADA Study

In 2005, the NTSB conducted a study examining how pipeline companies use SCADA systems to monitor and record operating data and evaluating the role of SCADA systems in leak detection in the hazardous liquid pipeline industry. Based on information from previous accidents investigated by the NTSB, survey results, and site visits, the NTSB identified five areas for potential improvement: display graphics, alarm management, controller training, controller fatigue, and leak detection systems. As a result, the NTSB issued five safety recommendations to PHMSA:

P-05-1

Require operators of hazardous liquid pipelines to follow the American Petroleum Institute's Recommended Practice 1165 for the use of graphics on Supervisory Control and Data Acquisition Screens. (Classified Closed—Acceptable Action on April 28, 2010)

P-05-2

Require pipeline companies to have a policy for the review/audit of alarms. (Classified Closed—Acceptable Action on April 28, 2010)

P-05-3

Require controller training to include simulator or non-computerized simulations for controller recognition of abnormal operating conditions, in particular, leak events. (Classified Closed—Acceptable Action on April 28, 2010)

P-05-4

Change the liquid accident reporting form (PHMSA F 700-1) and require operators to provide data related to controller fatigue. (Classified Closed—Acceptable Action on April 6, 2010)

P-05-5

Require operators to install computer-based leak detection systems on all lines unless engineering analysis determines that such a system is not necessary. (Classified Closed—Acceptable Alternate Action on May 6, 2010)

Recognizing the applicability of the liquid pipeline findings to the gas pipeline industry, PHMSA expanded the action taken for the liquid pipeline recommendations to the gas pipeline industry.

1.5.3 PHMSA and Control System Alarm Standards

The pipeline and process industries that rely on SCADA-type systems are challenged to design an alarm system that most effectively helps controllers detect leaks or other potential problems. The Columbia Gas strategy for determining how alarms and alerts were structured on the SCADA system was influenced by a new PHMSA regulation on control room management.[19] In 2009, PHMSA issued the control room management (CRM) regulations codified in 49 CFR 192.631 (gas) and 195.446 (liquid) to address human factors and other aspects of control room management for pipelines operated by SCADA systems. One intent of these rules was to ensure that pipeline controllers have sufficient time to analyze and react to alarms.

---

[19] The PHMSA regulations were developed as a result of NTSB recommendations from the SCADA study.

During the development of the CRM regulation, the International Society of Automation (ISA) was developing ANSI/ISA Standard 18.2, *Management of Alarm Systems for the Process Industries*.[20] The ANSI/ISA standard includes alarm management standards that are applicable to SCADA systems.[21] An alarm is defined as "an audible and/or visual means of indicating to the operator [controller] an equipment malfunction, process deviation, or abnormal condition requiring a response." The standard also discusses the number of alarms that can be safely managed by controllers over a range of time. Based on metrics that have been defined in the standard, between 150 and 300 alarms per day should be manageable by a single controller.

In response to the CRM regulations, Columbia Gas revised its SCADA system alarm management plan, including the safety-related alarms. Columbia Gas organized the SCADA system alarm screen display into three distinct sections: alarms, alerts, and communication outages. Conditions designated as alarms indicate that equipment or processes are outside of pipeline operator-defined, safety-related parameters. Conversely, alerts are indications that are not integral to safety-related parameters. For example, alerts indicate that conditions have changed, equipment or other monitoring variables are outside of the defined controlling parameters, or equipment, devices, or processes are not functioning as intended.

The Columbia Gas revisions to the SCADA system successfully reduced the number of alarms presented on the SCADA system alarm screen. The new configuration on the combined Charleston and Commonwealth alarm systems averaged 45 per day, or 2 alarms per hour, which is within the parameters identified in the ANSI/ISA 18.2-2009 standard.

Although Columbia Gas was successful in limiting the number of alarms on the SCADA system alarm screen, a significant number of indicators (or status information) were displayed as alerts. In a 12-hour shift, a gas controller monitoring both the Columbia and Charleston pipeline systems received an average of 1,145 alerts, or about one every 30 seconds. The gas controllers were responsible for acknowledging each of these alerts.

Columbia Gas relies on the controller to recognize an abnormal condition from the SCADA system alarms, alerts, or other system information. The Sissonville accident demonstrates the need to configure alerts to provide actionable information about the state of the pipeline system and the need for a timely and appropriate response. Without such information, the controller might not recognize that a safety-significant situation is developing or has occurred.

Although he had acknowledged the initial group of pressure-deviation alerts and several ensuing pressure alerts, the Columbia Gas controller did not recognize that a pressure decay trend had begun to develop. For multiple consecutive repeating alerts, the SCADA system should be capable of monitoring a series of alert conditions and present the data if a trend has developed. This would be a simple yet effective way to reduce the burden on the controller to remember or analyze a series of data outputs. A trend that is indicating an abnormal or unsafe

---

[20] ANSI is the American National Standards Institute. ISA is the International Society of Automation.

[21] Because the ISA-18.2 was being updated the same time PHMSA was developing its regulation, PHMSA chose not to adopt the ANSI/ISA standard while it was being revised. The applicable version was issued in 2009.

condition could be programmed to trigger an alarm condition that would notify the controller to examine the condition and take corrective action to resolve it. If the system had such provisions, it likely would have helped the controller to recognize the rupture before the Cabot controller called him. The NTSB concludes that providing automatic SCADA system trend data alerts will improve controller recognition of abnormal conditions.

1.6 Pipeline Corrosion

The soil surrounding and in contact with the buried pipe segment in the immediate area of the rupture was very rocky.[22] (See figure 6.) The rules for backfilling the trench when the pipe was installed cautioned only against damaging the pipe coating if the backfill material contained large rocks.

For submerged or buried pipelines, when the current from a cathodic protection system enters the exposed pipe surface, the pipe surface is protected from corrosion. If the exposed pipe surface is shielded (blocked) from the current flow, it is not protected and likely will corrode. A current shield is typically any barrier that prevents the protective current from reaching the exposed pipe surface. Various materials, such as tree roots, rocks, and disbonded dielectric coatings, can provide shielding. The NTSB concludes that the coarse rock backfill most likely damaged the external coating on the pipe and shielded the pipe from the cathodic protection current in the vicinity of the rupture.

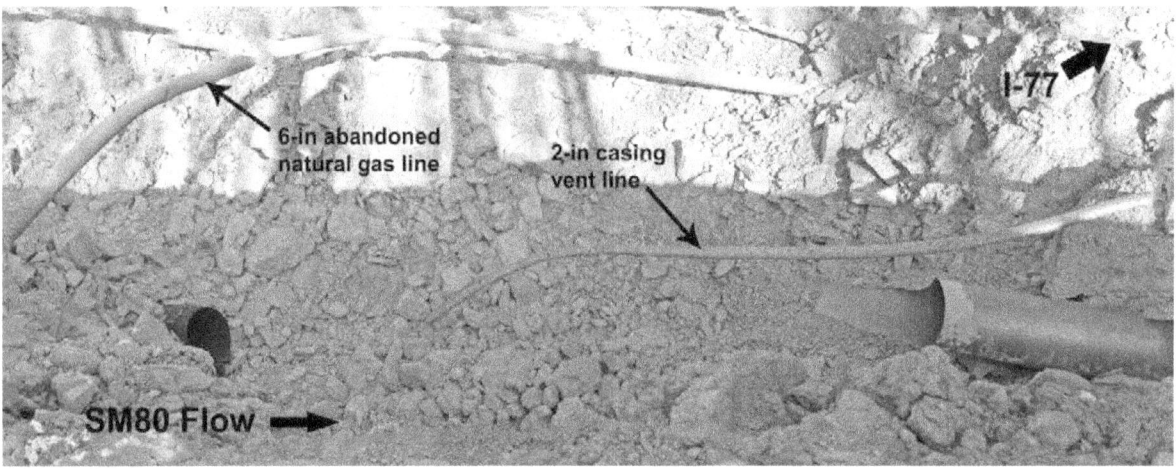

Figure 6. Ends of ruptured 20-inch SM-80 pipeline in rocky backfill.

The pipeline failure investigation began by excavating the ground past the upstream and downstream ends of the ruptured pipe joint. The ends were cut with a torch about 1 foot past the upstream and downstream girth welds. The two pipe pieces and the ejected pipe were shipped to

---

[22] The rules for design, fabrication, and construction of the 1967 vintage Line SM-80 pipe are contained in the American Standard Code for Pressure Piping, ASA B31.8, *Gas Transmission and Distribution Piping Systems*, 1963.

the NTSB Materials Laboratory in Washington, DC. Examination of the sections indicated that the longitudinal seam in the ruptured pipe was at about the 1 o'clock position, looking east (downstream).

The NTSB Materials Laboratory examined three pieces of steel pipe from Line SM-80:

- The ejected piece of pipe that ruptured, about 20 feet long

- One piece of pipe about 11 feet long, which was immediately downstream (east) of the ruptured piece

- One piece of pipe about 8 feet long, which was immediately upstream (west) of the ruptured piece

Laboratory measurements indicated that the ruptured pipe joint was 37 feet 8 1/2 inches long and 20 1/2 inches in diameter. The longitudinal fracture was 20 feet 3 inches long. (See figure 7.) Comparing the fracture features of the upstream and downstream ends of the pipe in the crater and the position of the longitudinal seam in the ruptured segment, investigators determined that the longitudinal fracture was near the bottom of the pipe.

The pipe wall thickness was measured along the longitudinal fracture using calipers and on a two-dimensional grid on the inner wall surface using an ultrasonic thickness gauge. The lowest caliper reading was 0.078 inch taken on the upstream side of the lateral tear. The caliper readings indicated that the corroded area extended about 6 feet along the longitudinal fracture. The ultrasonic thickness measurements showed a similar extent of wall thinning in the longitudinal direction. The extent of wall thinning along the longitudinal direction was greatest near the tear and extended about 26 inches. The lowest ultrasonic thickness reading was 0.103 inch (37 percent of the original thickness), taken 1 inch upstream of the tear.

Figure 7. Ejected ruptured pipe.

The ruptured pipe joint was covered with a green polymer coating about 0.010 inch thick. A coal tar enamel coating was applied on top of the green coating along parts of the top and sides of the pipe. Coal tar coverage was not uniform, and the green coating was disbonded in some areas. (See figure 8.) The uniform thickness and relatively smooth surface of the green coating was consistent with application at a factory. The rough appearance of the coal tar was consistent with application in the field.

Figure 8. Underside of pipe upstream of rupture exhibiting primarily uncoated pipe. Boundaries of uncoated portion of pipe are indicated by yellow arrows.

The coating coverage varied over the surface of the pipe. Many regions, primarily along the bottom of the pipe, had no protective coating. In other regions, primarily along the sides, the pipe was covered by the green coating but not the coal tar. Along the top of the pipe, the green coating was generally covered by coal tar.

Wall thickness measurements were also taken in areas where the green coating adhered to the pipe and the pipe had not corroded. On the upstream pipe piece, the average wall thickness was 0.278 inch. On the downstream pipe piece, the average wall thickness was 0.283 inch. The wall thickness of the uncoated pipe regions along the 6:00 position on the upstream and downstream pipe pieces was measured using the ultrasonic thickness gauge at 6-inch intervals. On the upstream pipe piece, the wall thickness readings varied from 0.271 inch to 0.279 inch. On the downstream pipe piece, the wall thickness readings varied from 0.276 inch to 0.284 inch.

Visual examination of the longitudinal fracture after cleaning showed an area of significant external corrosion damage that was 6 feet 3 inches long and 29 inches wide. (See figure 9.)

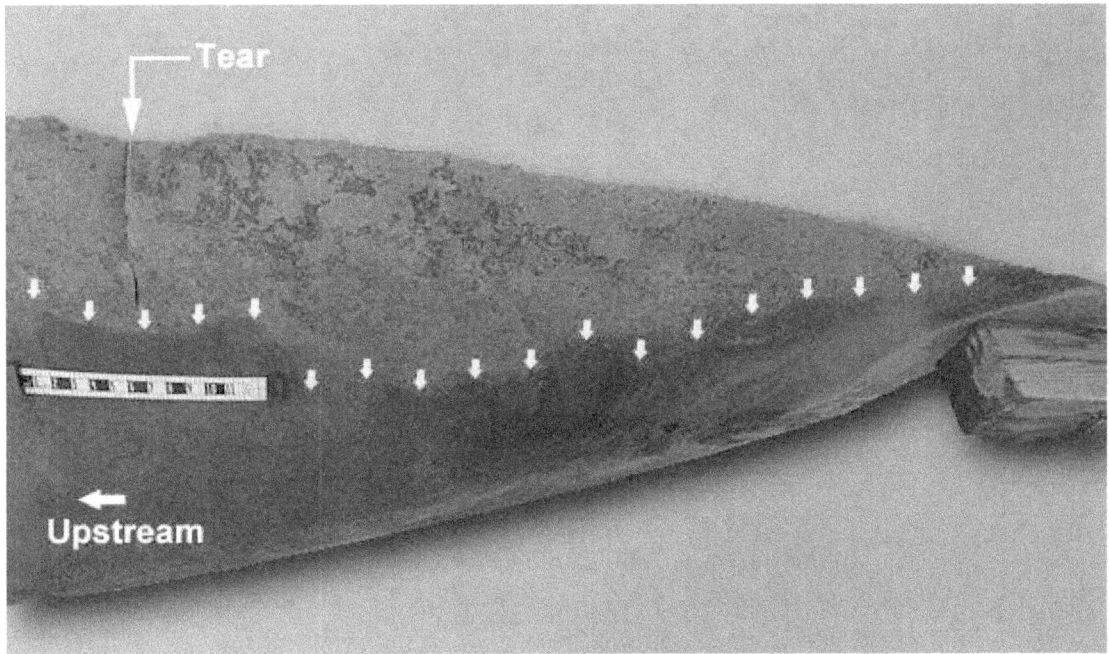

Figure 9. External corrosion along longitudinal fracture, with boundary of visible corrosion indicated with arrows.

Visual examination of the fracture surfaces determined that the rupture initiated immediately upstream of the lateral tear. The fracture surface had a rough and irregular appearance, features that are consistent with a ductile overstress fracture. The initiation site is shown in figure 10.

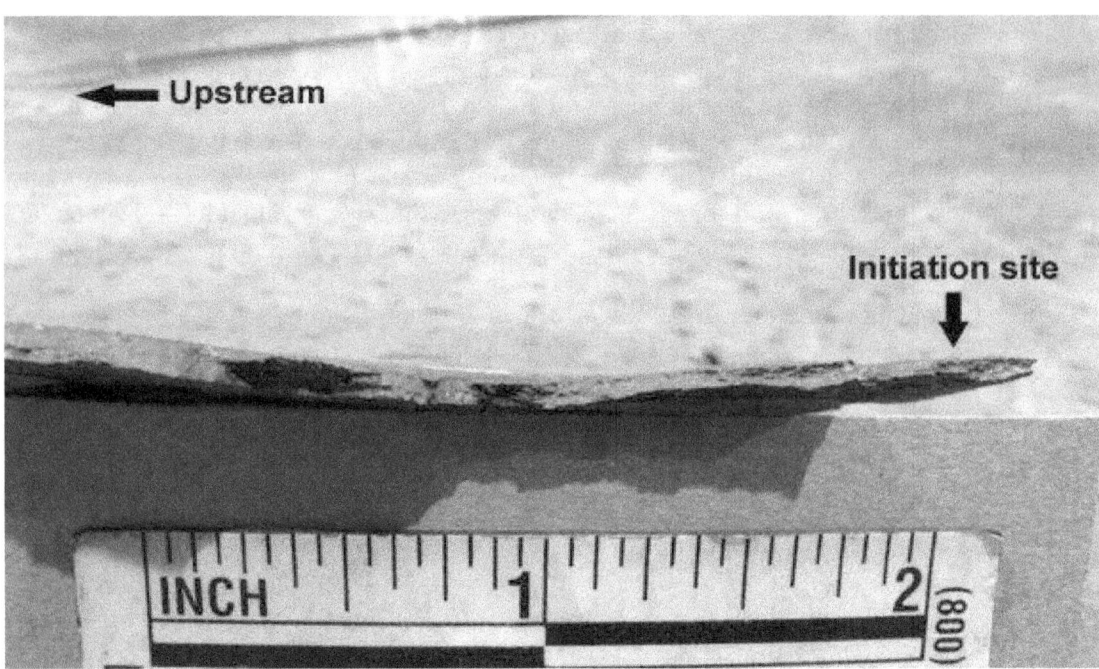

Figure 10. Longitudinal fracture surface on upstream side of lateral tear.

Test specimens were cut and prepared for tensile testing and chemical analysis. The average yield strength (0.5 percent elongation method) was 68,000 pounds per square inch (psi). The average tensile strength was 88,000 psi. The average elongation was 27 percent. Test results show that the mechanical properties and chemical composition of the pipe were in accordance with the API Standard 5L grade X60 specification.

The burst pressure of the pipe was estimated using the corroded pipe wall thickness data, nominal wall thickness, and measured yield strength (table 1) and nominal yield strength (table 2) following the procedure outlined in ASME B31G-2009 (ASME 2009).

Table 1. Calculated burst pressure values following ASME B31G-2009 and using the measured yield strength of 68,000 psi.

Evaluation Method	Estimated Burst Pressure, psig
B31G	770
Modified B31G	1039
Effective Area Method	1117

Table 2. Calculated burst pressure values following ASME B31G-2009 and using the specified minimum yield strength of API Standard 5L grade X60 pipe of 60,000 psi.

Evaluation Method	Estimated Burst Pressure, psig
B31G	680
Modified B31G	932
Effective Area Method	1002

The calculated rupture pressures are consistent with a ductile overstress failure caused by external corrosion. The pipe ruptured at 929 psig, compared to the rupture pressure calculated using measured mechanical property values that ranges from 770 psig to 1,117 psig.

The pipeline coating provided the primary means of corrosion protection. The cathodic protection was intended to protect the exposed pipe in the areas of coating damage, such as cracked or chipped coating. However, when the cathodic protection current is prevented from reaching an area of exposed metal because of shielding by rocks or disbonded coating, the current cannot protect the pipe, and the unprotected area will corrode.

The ruptured pipe segment contained areas of uncoated metal where the coating had disbonded and cracked. There was no external corrosion in those areas, because the cathodic protection likely worked as it was intended. However, more than 30 square feet of the pipe was heavily corroded on the outside surface, as shown in figures 9 and 10. This indicates that the cathodic protection system did not work in the area, likely because of localized shielding caused by the rock backfill. Based on the laboratory findings and field observation of the rupture area, the NTSB concludes that Line SM-80 failed because of severe wall thinning caused by external corrosion. The corrosion occurred because the external protective coating allowed moisture to come in contact with the pipe and the large, coarse rock backfill adjacent to the pipeline blocked the cathodic protection current from the exposed pipe.

1.7 Columbia Gas Corrosion Mitigation Program

The external corrosion protection plan is described in Columbia Pipeline Group Plan 70.01.01. For Columbia Gas steel pipelines, external corrosion protection is achieved by use of external coating supplemented with cathodic protection. All three pipelines in the SM-80 system were coated and were protected by an impressed current cathodic protection system.

For Line SM-80, the cathodic protection readings taken from the closest test station in the vicinity of the rupture (about 100 feet) over the past 10 years (2003–2012) were satisfactory. Similar readings for Line SM-86 and Line SM-86 Loop from 2005 to 2012 were also satisfactory.

1.7.1 In-Line Inspections

Line SM-80 was not in an HCA at the rupture location, so it was not required to be assessed by in-line inspection (ILI) or any other integrity assessment method.[23] The two adjacent, larger-diameter lines were designated to be in an HCA, and they were inspected using ILI. Both had a history of corrosion damage and resulting repairs.

Line SM-86 Loop had an ILI on February 10, 2009, using a geometry (caliper/deformation) tool and on March 10, 2009, using a high-resolution magnetic flux leakage tool. Anomalies were detected on Line SM-86 within about 500 feet of the Line SM-80 rupture.[24] The data show that there were 161 external metal loss features with 10 percent or more wall thickness loss (nominal wall thickness of 0.385 inch). Of those features, 15 indicated 20 to 30 percent wall loss. The remainder were between 10 and 20 percent wall loss. None required repair.

Line SM-86 was inspected on June 25, 2009, using a geometry tool and on June 26, 2009, using a high-resolution magnetic flux leakage tool. The data contained 63 anomalies on Line SM-86 within about 500 feet of the Line SM-80 rupture that had depths up to 40 percent of the wall thickness. Forty-eight anomalies were between 10 and 20 percent of the wall thickness depth. However, none required repair.

After the June 26, 2009, ILI inspection, an indication 8.9 inches long and 28.8 inches wide with 47 percent wall loss was excavated and repaired.[25] Another indication, 7.9 inches long and 11.4 inches wide with 41 percent wall loss, was also repaired.

Documentation provided by Columbia Gas did not show whether any of this ILI information was provided to personnel responsible for Line SM-80 corrosion protection and, if so, how it was used. All three pipelines in the SM-80 system are of comparable age. The data obtained during the 2009 ILIs clearly show that both Line SM-86 and Line SM-86 Loop suffered from various degrees of external corrosion damage even though they were coated and had cathodic protection. This information should have been considered in evaluating the condition of Line SM-80. The NTSB concludes that the corrosion damage discovered in 2009 during the ILIs of the other two pipelines in the SM-80 system was not adequately considered by Columbia Gas when it evaluated corrosion mitigation approaches for Line SM-80. The NTSB further concludes that had Line SM-80 been inspected using ILI or pressure tested after ILI data for Line SM-86 and Line SM-86 Loop were evaluated, the inspection results likely would have revealed the

---

[23] In 1988, Columbia Gas performed an ILI on Line SM-80 to determine whether to replace the uncoated pipe. The ILI tool reported only anomalies with a depth that exceeded 50 percent of the wall thickness in the segment involved in the December 2012 accident.

[24] An *anomaly* is metal loss, including general corrosion or pinholes, linear (crack) indications, gouges, dents, or other physical damage either on the surface of a pipe or in the pipe wall. The decision to repair a pipeline to remove an anomaly is based on a written procedure that rates anomalies based on depth, length, and width and proximity to other anomalies.

[25] A *indication* is a signal from an ILI that is used to identify an *anomaly* (abnormality, variation, defect) in a pipeline, which may be further evaluated to classify the anomaly as a certain *feature* (weight loss, crack, girth weld) and classified or characterized as an anomaly, an imperfection, or a component.

severe wall loss at the rupture location, and the in-service rupture of Line SM-80 could have been prevented. The NTSB recommends that Columbia Gas establish a procedure to ensure that all integrity-related information gathered for pipelines located in HCAs is considered in the risk assessments and IM of other pipelines not located in HCAs.

1.7.2 Close Interval Surveys

A close interval survey (CIS) to assess the condition of the pipe coating and the level of cathodic protection is typically conducted by walking along a pipeline and measuring pipe-to-soil voltage (potentials) every few feet. The readings are compared with the expected cathodic protection level, and locations that fail to meet the expected level are identified and evaluated for mitigation.

A CIS was performed on the SM-80 system in 1995. According to Columbia Gas, 6 areas on Line SM-80, 5 areas on Line SM-86, and 16 areas on Line SM-86 Loop did not meet the expected level. A CIS was performed on portions of Line SM-86 in 2004 and 2005 while a new CIS data logger was being tested. Data revealed that 17 areas required corrective action. The remedial measures included installation of additional cathodic protection systems, investigation and elimination of potential interference sources, and pipe recoating. None of the mitigated areas were near the Line SM-80 rupture location.

A Columbia Gas corrosion technician noted that a CIS provides useful information about the condition of pipeline coating. However, the Columbia Gas director of IM stated that "coating holidays and areas of potentially inadequate cathodic protection may not be detected if the area is electrically shielded from cathodic protection current."[26] Although Columbia Gas was aware of this limitation of cathodic protection and CIS and was aware in 2009 that the adjacent pipelines in the SM-80 system experienced external corrosion at many locations, the company did not use any other tools or techniques to ensure the integrity of Line SM-80. A variety of tools, such as ILI, CIS, and pressure testing, are available to pipeline operators for evaluating pipeline integrity, each with advantages and limitations. For example, pressure testing requires taking the pipeline out of service, filling it with water, and draining and drying the pipe. Close interval surveys measure the cathodic protection voltage every few feet along a specific length of the pipe, so it does not cover 100 percent of the pipe and does not detect shielding caused by rocks or other material. Digging to expose the pipe provides access to the pipe surface to conduct visual and other examinations, but it is costly and may damage the pipe coating. The advantages and limitations of the evaluation methods need to be considered by pipeline operators when evaluating pipeline integrity to ensure safe operation.

---

[26] A *holiday* is a hole in the protective coating material that can allow moisture to come in contact with the pipe surface.

1.8 Integrity Management

1.8.1 Pipelines Close to Highways

PHMSA promulgated the IM rule for natural gas transmission pipelines on January 14, 2004, following the enactment of the Pipeline Safety Improvement Act of 2002.[27] The IM rule, at 49 CFR 192.903(1)(iii), requires pipeline operators to identify HCAs along a pipeline based on a potential impact radius (PIR), which is a function of pipe diameter and pressure. The buildings within the PIR circle that are intended for human occupancy are counted. If the number is 20 or more, the area is classified as an HCA.

During the comment period for the IM rule, several commenters argued that additional infrastructure facilities, such as interstate interchanges, bridges, certain railway facilities, electric transmission substations, and drinking water plants, should be included in the HCA definition. However, in deciding to exclude these additional areas from the HCAs, PHMSA stated the following:

> When we issued the final rule defining these areas, we agreed that impacts to critical infrastructure could have detrimental impact but that such impacts would not likely include death or serious injury. A major purpose of the integrity management rule is to focus the highest level of [pipeline] operator attention on those portions of its pipeline that can have the most severe safety consequences, i.e., can cause death and injury. (*Federal Register* 2003, 69785)

According to the Public Service Commission of West Virginia (PSC) no highway fatality or injury resulted from a pipeline accident in West Virginia from January 1, 2000, to April 12, 2013; the PSC added that in that time, only two pipeline incidents involving motor vehicles occurred, and they were on distribution systems.[28] The PSC further stated that West Virginia has only 7 locations where pipelines cross interstate highways (including the Line SM-80 I-77 crossing), 2 locations where pipelines cross limited access highways, and 87 locations where interstate pipelines cross roads.

According to PHMSA, there are 7,105 locations nationwide where natural gas transmission pipelines cross divided and/or interstate highways. Of these 4,282 are in HCAs. PHMSA also reported that within the United States, 5,804 miles of gas transmission pipelines lie within 660 feet of major highways. Of these, 3,427 miles of pipelines are within HCAs, and PHMSA stated that it is possible that some of the remaining 2,377 miles of pipelines might already be covered by IM plans.

The NTSB reviewed the history of pipeline accidents near interstate highways that occurred between January 2000 and April 2013. On December 14, 2007, a pipeline ruptured near

---

[27] The Pipeline Safety Improvement Act of 2002, Pub. L. 107-355, was signed into law on December 17, 2002, and codified at 49 U.S.C. 60109.

[28] PSC April 12, 2013, e-mail to NTSB staff.

Interstate 20 in Delhi, Louisiana, killing a man who was driving on the highway and injuring his passenger.[29] On May 4, 2009, an 18-inch-diameter natural gas transmission pipeline owned and operated by Florida Gas Transmission Company ruptured in Palm City, Florida (NTSB 2013). The rupture was located in the right-of-way between Interstate 95 and the Florida Turnpike. There was no ignition, but two injuries occurred when the driver of a car on the interstate lost control of the car.

The Sissonville pipeline rupture caused major damage to I-77. An intense fire raged directly across the interstate for nearly an hour. Had the accident occurred during commuting hours, when traffic would have been significant, severe or fatal injuries could have occurred. Both the Sissonville and the Palm City accidents show the vulnerability of highways, or principal arterial roadways, that are close to high-pressure pipelines and the threat that proximity poses to the safety of people and property.[30] The NTSB is concerned that gas transmission pipelines in proximity to arterial roadways are exempted from HCA consideration by PHMSA. Both the Sissonville and the Palm City, Florida (NTSB 2013), accidents show the consequences of pipeline ruptures to the nation's arterial roadways. Sudden closure of arterial roadways for several hours can significantly affect commuters, first responders, and US commerce. Therefore, the NTSB concludes that if pipelines in proximity to highways had been included in the HCA classification, the ruptured area of Line SM-80 would have been covered by the IM regulation and would have been evaluated. Furthermore, the NTSB concludes that the consequences of a pipeline rupture in proximity to an arterial roadway are similar to the consequences of a pipeline rupture near structures for human occupancy, as currently addressed in an HCA. The NTSB recommends that PHMSA revise 49 CFR Section 903, Subpart O, *Gas Transmission Pipeline Integrity Management*, to add principal arterial roadways including interstates, other freeways and expressways, and other principal arterial roadways as defined in the Federal Highway Administration's *Highway Functional Classification Concepts, Criteria and Procedures* to the list of "identified sites" that establish an HCA.

1.8.2 Columbia Gas Integrity Management Program

The Columbia Gas IM program is integrated into other functional groups within Columbia Gas including the project, operations, and maintenance teams. In 2009, Columbia Gas established an integrity steering team that is a cross-functional team responsible and accountable for the IM program and that reports to the president of operations and engineering and the senior vice president of operations. The integrity steering team is responsible for developing and coordinating a comprehensive IM program. The team is responsible for defining and leading the

---

[29] PHMSA staff, e-mail message to NTSB staff, April 19, 2013.

[30] *Principal arterial roadways,* or *arterial roadways,* as defined in the Federal Highway Administration's *Highway Functional Classification Concepts, Criteria and Procedures*, are designed and constructed to maximize their mobility function. They include interstates, other freeways and expressways, and other principal arterials. Other freeways and expressways "have directional travel lanes that are usually separated by some type of physical barrier, and their access and egress points are limited to on- and off-ramp locations or a very limited number of at-grade intersections" Other principal arterial roadways "serve major centers of metropolitan areas, provide a high degree of mobility, and can also provide mobility through rural areas." They are not access-controlled and may be accessed by driveways to specific areas and intersections with other roadways.

companywide system integrity efforts to mitigate identified risk, assure regulatory compliance, and effectively execute the IM program. The Columbia Gas IM program involves identifying HCAs along its pipeline system, identifying threats and ranking risks, conducting assessments, and taking appropriate action to ensure the integrity of pipelines in the HCA. Additionally, in 2010, Columbia Gas conducted risk assessments for the entire gas transmission pipeline system.

Pipeline regulations addressing internal and external corrosion monitoring and mitigation are risk based. Class 3 and Class 4 locations and Class 1 and Class 2 HCA locations have a higher population density, resulting in greater risk to the public, and therefore the regulations addressing corrosion are more stringent. The population densities in Class 1 and Class 2 areas not containing any HCAs are lower, and the pipeline regulations for evaluating pipeline integrity in those areas are less stringent.

Threat identification along with risk assessment and management is part of the overall IM program. The risk management team reviews the risk management results to identify those segments that require additional preventive and mitigative measures to manage the threats on the particular pipeline segment. The team also reviews the risk drivers and threats from the risk management reports and identifies additional potential preventive and mitigative measures.

For preventive and mitigative measures that are identified as operational activities, the risk management team coordinates activities with the operations team leaders to ensure proper actions are taken and the actions are recorded and updated in the Columbia Gas work management system records. The risk management team develops the actions that need to be taken as a part of the Columbia Gas IM program, and the IM or the operations team carries out the activities. Coordination is essential to ensure the proper action is taken and the action is part of the Columbia Gas work management system records that are audited by the PSC.

Columbia Gas conducts risk assessments annually, or more frequently if significant events, such as an accident or poor inspection readings, trigger an interim assessment. The interim assessment identifies risk level changes in the model. Events such as the installation of new facilities, changes to HCAs, changes to the risk model, or class changes can trigger an interim risk assessment. Relative risk scores are calculated through a series of algorithms developed by Columbia Gas, and higher scores indicate higher relative risk. The relative risk score of 13.45 near the rupture location was one of the top two scores for Line SM-80. According to Columbia Gas, the segments in its system with the highest risk typically have scores above 20.

Columbia Gas uses risk management to identify and quantify threats to pipeline safety and evaluates pipelines in HCAs and those not in HCAs by using various risk-based metrics. The information is used to prioritize pipeline segments based on the risk and the threats they are exposed to and to identify mitigation strategies to lower pipeline safety risk. As discussed in section 1.7.1, Columbia Gas had no records to show whether ILI information from Lines SM-86 and SM-86 Loop was considered to identify the external corrosion threats to Line SM-80.

The PIR circles for each pipeline in the SM-80 system at the rupture location are shown in figure 11. Each pipeline is evaluated individually to determine its HCA location. Pipeline interconnectivity, proximity to other pipelines, and any overlapping PIR circles do not impact HCA determinations.

Based on regulatory criteria, only Lines SM-86 and SM-86 Loop were in HCAs and covered by the IM regulation. Maintaining the integrity of Line SM-80 was the responsibility of the Corrosion Control department until 2010. In 2010, Columbia Gas implemented a new risk tool that allowed risk to be calculated throughout the pipeline system. The other two lines were in HCAs, so they were under the more stringent risk management plan.

1.9 Postaccident Corrective Actions

As a result this accident, PHMSA issued corrective action order (CAO) CPF No.1-2012-1025H to Columbia Gas on December 20, 2012. The CAO required Columbia Gas to develop written plans for specific actions, and the plans were required to be approved by PHMSA before any work could start. Some of the actions the CAO required Columbia Gas to perform were the following:

- Conduct an ILI of Line SM-80 using a high-resolution deformation and metal loss tool and excavate, investigate, and repair anomalies as if the line were in an HCA.

- Perform CIS, investigate, and correct deficiencies.

- Assess the integrity of the coating using direct current voltage gradient or alternating current voltage gradient surveys and correct any identified deficiencies.

In response to the CAO, Columbia Gas replaced several pipe segments in Line SM-80 with new 20-inch-diameter, 0.375-inch-thick wall, API Standard 5L grade X65 fusion-bonded epoxy mill-coated steel pipe and pressure tested the new segments to between 2,024 psig and 2,438 psig (83 to 100 percent of specified minimum yield strength). For a 1,000 psig MAOP pipeline, this test pressure translates to 202 to 243 percent of MAOP. Columbia Gas hydrostatically tested the pipe at a minimum test pressure of 2,438 psig.

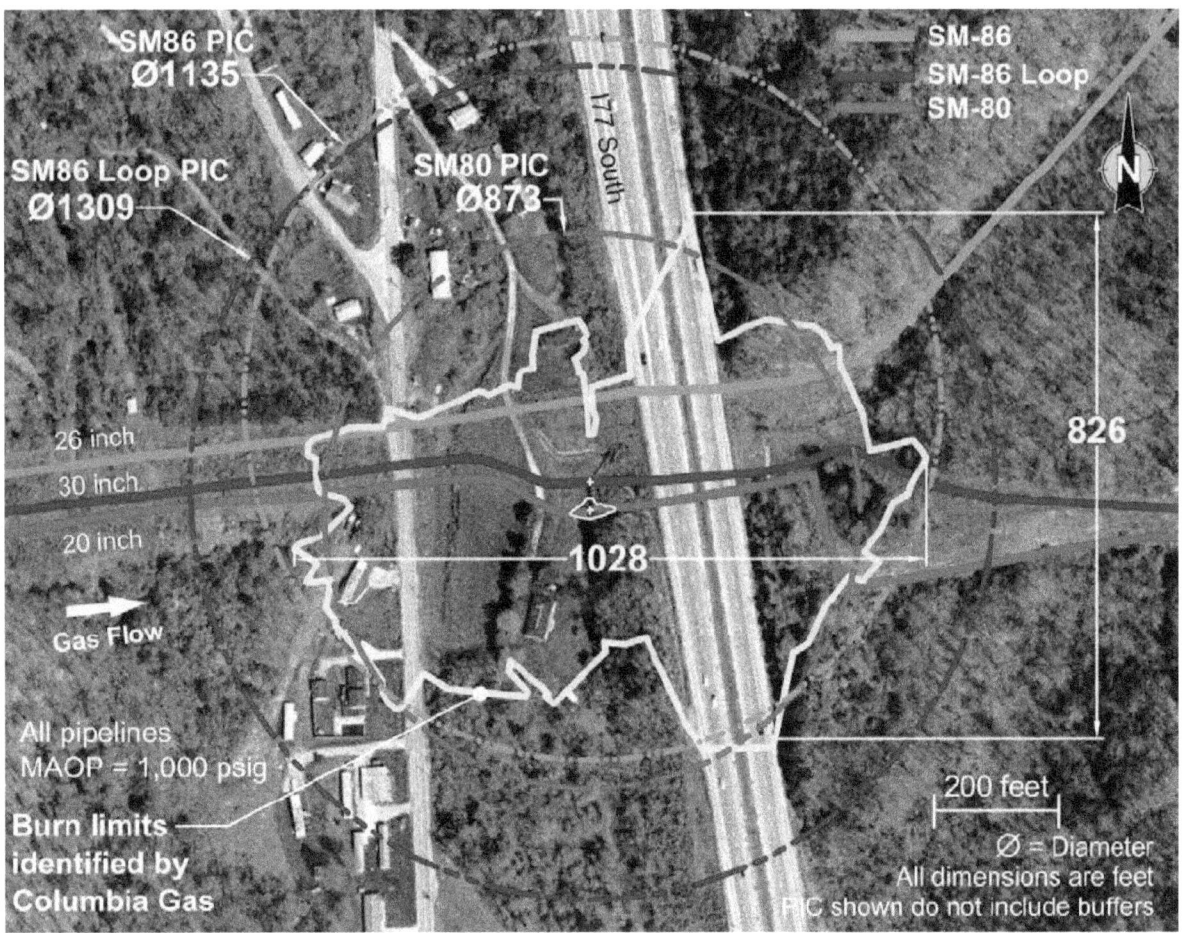

Figure 11. Potential impact radius circles for each pipeline in SM-80 system at rupture location.

The Columbia Gas plan included an ILI inspection and a CIS of Line SM-80. The 2013 ILI data identified eight external and two internal metal loss anomalies in the line. The smallest external metal loss anomaly was 9.0 inches long and 49.5 inches wide with 24 percent wall loss, and the largest external metal loss anomaly was 23.2 inches long and 62.6 inches wide with 29 percent wall loss (nominal wall 0.25 inch). Some dent anomalies were also reported. All work orders issued to correct the unacceptable anomalies on Line SM-80 were completed by October 2013.

2. Conclusions

2.1 Findings

1. Third-party direct pipeline impact damage was not a factor in this accident.

2. The controller was experienced and qualified, fit for duty, not physically fatigued, and not under the influence of illicit drugs or alcohol on the day of the accident.

3. Line SM-80 ruptured at 12:41 p.m.

4. Despite the many pressure deviation alerts occurring on the system over more than 12 minutes, the Columbia Gas Transmission Corporation controller did not recognize the significance of the situation or begin to shut down the system until after the Cabot controller called him.

5. The Columbia Gas Transmission Corporation supervisory control and data acquisition system alerts did not provide useful, meaningful information to the controller to assist him in determining the operating condition of the pipeline.

6. Providing automatic supervisory control and data acquisition system trend data alerts will improve controller recognition of abnormal conditions.

7. Strategically placed automatic shutoff values or remote controlled valves would have isolated the three pipelines and shortened the duration of the intense fire.

8. The coarse rock backfill most likely damaged the external coating on the pipe and shielded the pipe from the cathodic protection current in the vicinity of the rupture.

9. Line SM-80 failed because of severe wall thinning caused by external corrosion.

10. The corrosion damage discovered in 2009 during the in-line inspections of the other two pipelines in the SM-80 system was not adequately considered by Columbia Gas Transmission Corporation when it evaluated corrosion mitigation approaches for Line SM-80.

11. Had Line SM-80 been inspected using in-line inspection or pressure tested after in-line inspection data for Line SM-86 and Line SM-86 Loop were evaluated, the inspection results likely would have revealed the severe wall loss at the rupture location, and the in-service rupture of Line SM-80 could have been prevented.

12. If pipelines in proximity to highways had been included in the high consequence area classification, the ruptured area of Line SM-80 would have been covered by the integrity management regulation and would have been evaluated.

13. The consequences of a pipeline rupture in proximity to an arterial roadway are similar to the consequences of a pipeline rupture near structures for human occupancy, as currently addressed in a high consequence area.

2.2. Probable Cause

The National Transportation Safety Board determines that the probable cause of the pipeline rupture was (1) external corrosion of the pipe wall due to deteriorated coating and ineffective cathodic protection and (2) the failure to detect the corrosion because the pipeline was not inspected or tested after 1988. Contributing to the poor condition of the corrosion protection systems was the rocky backfill used around the buried pipe. Contributing to the delay in the controller's recognition of the rupture was Columbia Gas Transmission Corporation management's inadequate configuration of the alerts in the supervisory control and data acquisition system. Contributing to the delay in isolating the rupture was the lack of automatic shutoff or remote control valves.

3. Recommendations

As a result of this investigation, the National Transportation Safety Board makes the following new safety recommendations:

To the Pipeline and Hazardous Materials Safety Administration:

Revise Title 49 *Code of Federal Regulations* Section 903, Subpart O, *Gas Transmission Pipeline Integrity Management*, to add principal arterial roadways including interstates, other freeways and expressways, and other principal arterial roadways as defined in the Federal Highway Administration's *Highway Functional Classification Concepts, Criteria and Procedures* to the list of "identified sites" that establish a high consequence area. (P-14-1)

To Columbia Gas Transmission Corporation:

Implement a process for selecting alert setpoints, and provide guidance to pipeline controllers on the expected alert response time, ways to evaluate the significance of alerts, and actions the controller must take in response to those alerts. (P-14-2)

Modify your supervisory control and data acquisition system to (1) provide the controller with operating parameter trend data that can be used to evaluate the significance of a system change and (2) assign an alarm function to trends that are likely significant system malfunctions and therefore require immediate action by the controller. (P-14-3)

Establish a procedure to ensure that all integrity-related information gathered for pipelines located in high consequence areas is considered in the risk assessments and integrity management of other pipelines not located in high consequence areas. (P-14-4)

BY THE NATIONAL TRANSPORTATION SAFETY BOARD

DEBORAH A.P. HERSMAN
Chairman

ROBERT L. SUMWALT
Member

CHRISTOPHER A. HART
Vice Chairman

MARK R. ROSEKIND
Member

EARL F. WEENER
Member

Adopted: February 19, 2014

4. Appendixes

4.1 Appendix A: Investigation

The National Response Center was notified of the rupture of Columbia Gas Transmission Corporation's natural gas transmission pipeline at 1:24 p.m. on December 11, 2012. NTSB Member Robert Sumwalt and six investigators launched to the accident scene.

On January 20, 2013, NTSB Chairman Deborah Hersman testified before a field hearing of the Senate Committee on Commerce, Science, and Transportation in Charleston, West Virginia, regarding the NTSB's ongoing investigation of the pipeline rupture and fire in Sissonville and the safety risks posed by the transportation of oil and natural gas by pipeline. Her statement described to the Committee the pipeline that ruptured in Sissonville, the impact of the rupture and subsequent fire, and actions taken immediately afterward. She also briefed the Committee on key NTSB findings and recommendations as the result of its past investigations of major pipeline accidents.

Parties to the investigation were Pipeline and Hazardous Materials Safety Administration; Public Service Commission of West Virginia; Columbia Gas Transmission Corporation; Kanawha County Sheriff's Office; and West Virginia State Police, South Charleston Detachment.

4.2 Appendix B: Timeline

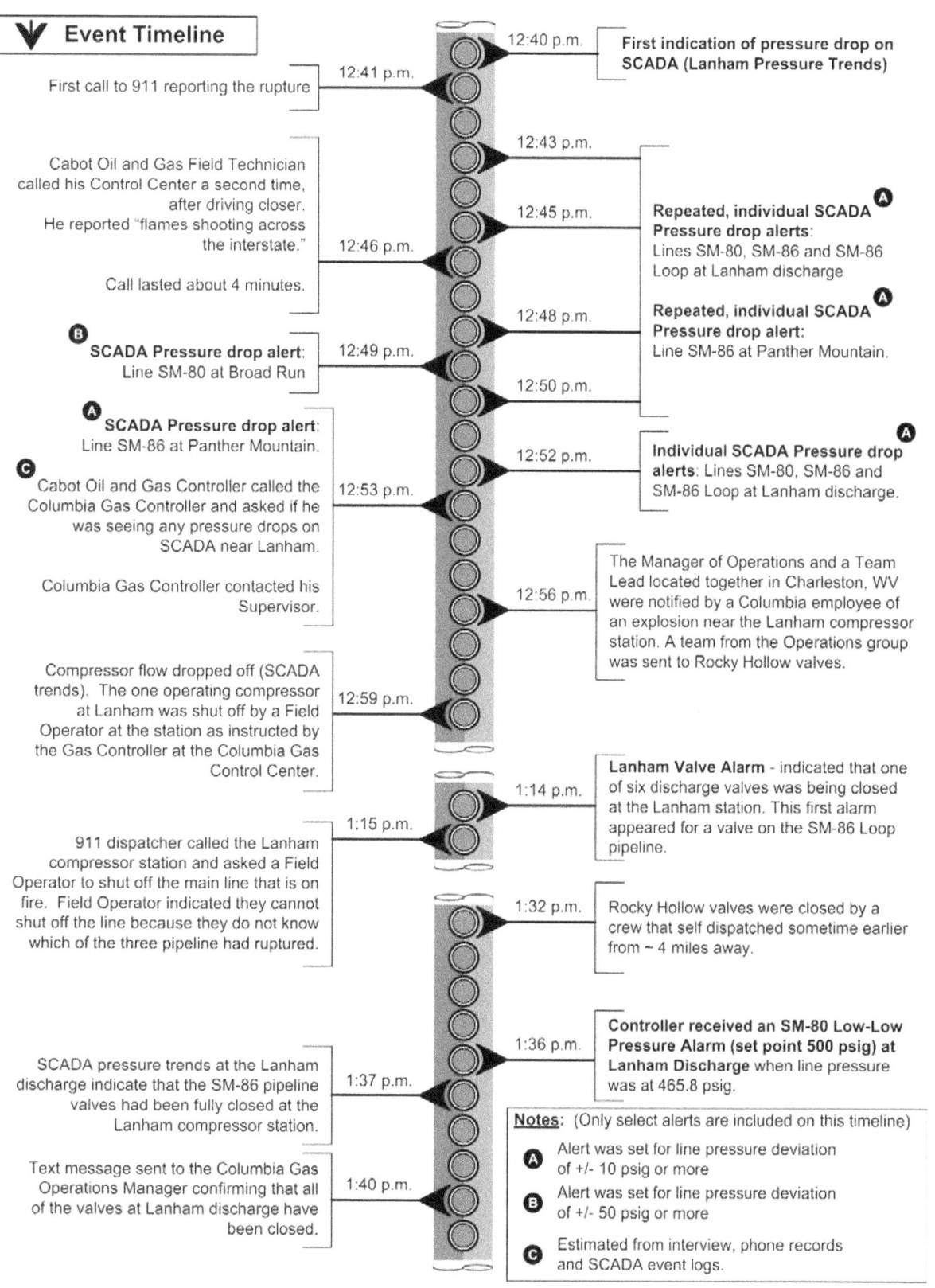

Event Timeline

First call to 911 reporting the rupture — 12:41 p.m.

Cabot Oil and Gas Field Technician called his Control Center a second time, after driving closer. He reported "flames shooting across the interstate."

Call lasted about 4 minutes. — 12:46 p.m.

B SCADA Pressure drop alert: Line SM-80 at Broad Run — 12:49 p.m.

A SCADA Pressure drop alert: Line SM-86 at Panther Mountain.

C Cabot Oil and Gas Controller called the Columbia Gas Controller and asked if he was seeing any pressure drops on SCADA near Lanham. — 12:53 p.m.

Columbia Gas Controller contacted his Supervisor.

Compressor flow dropped off (SCADA trends). The one operating compressor at Lanham was shut off by a Field Operator at the station as instructed by the Gas Controller at the Columbia Gas Control Center. — 12:59 p.m.

911 dispatcher called the Lanham compressor station and asked a Field Operator to shut off the main line that is on fire. Field Operator indicated they cannot shut off the line because they do not know which of the three pipeline had ruptured. — 1:15 p.m.

SCADA pressure trends at the Lanham discharge indicate that the SM-86 pipeline valves had been fully closed at the Lanham compressor station. — 1:37 p.m.

Text message sent to the Columbia Gas Operations Manager confirming that all of the valves at Lanham discharge have been closed. — 1:40 p.m.

12:40 p.m. — **First indication of pressure drop on SCADA (Lanham Pressure Trends)**

12:43 p.m.

12:45 p.m. — **Repeated, individual SCADA** **A** **Pressure drop alerts:** Lines SM-80, SM-86 and SM-86 Loop at Lanham discharge

12:48 p.m. — **Repeated, individual SCADA** **A** **Pressure drop alert:** Line SM-86 at Panther Mountain.

12:50 p.m.

12:52 p.m. — **Individual SCADA Pressure drop** **A** **alerts:** Lines SM-80, SM-86 and SM-86 Loop at Lanham discharge.

12:56 p.m. — The Manager of Operations and a Team Lead located together in Charleston, WV were notified by a Columbia employee of an explosion near the Lanham compressor station. A team from the Operations group was sent to Rocky Hollow valves.

1:14 p.m. — **Lanham Valve Alarm** - indicated that one of six discharge valves was being closed at the Lanham station. This first alarm appeared for a valve on the SM-86 Loop pipeline.

1:32 p.m. — Rocky Hollow valves were closed by a crew that self dispatched sometime earlier from ~ 4 miles away.

1:36 p.m. — **Controller received an SM-80 Low-Low Pressure Alarm (set point 500 psig) at Lanham Discharge** when line pressure was at 465.8 psig.

Notes: (Only select alerts are included on this timeline)

A Alert was set for line pressure deviation of +/- 10 psig or more

B Alert was set for line pressure deviation of +/- 50 psig or more

C Estimated from interview, phone records and SCADA event logs.

39

References

ASME (American Society of Mechanical Engineers). 2009. *Manual for Determining the Remaining Strength of Corroded Pipelines: Supplement to ASME B31 Code for Pressure Piping*, B31G–2009. New York: ASME.

Federal Register. 2009. Vol. 60, no. 97 (December 3).

----. 2003. Vol. 68, no. 240 (December 15).

Federal Highway Administration. 2013. *Highway Functional Classification: Concepts, Criteria and Procedures*, FHWA-PL-13-026. Washington, DC: Federal Highway Administration, US Department of Transportation.

NTSB (National Transportation Safety Board). 2013. *Pipeline Rupture and Gas Release, Palm City, Florida, May 4, 2009*, PAB-13/01. Washington, DC: NTSB.

----. 2011. *Pacific Gas and Electric Company Natural Gas Transmission Pipeline Rupture and Fire, San Bruno, California, September 9, 2010*, PAR-11/01. Washington, DC: NTSB.

----. 2007. *Anhydrous Ammonia Pipeline Rupture, Kingman, Kansas, October 27, 2004*, PAB-07/02. Washington, DC: NTSB.

----. 1999. *Hazardous Liquid Petroleum Products Overpressure Rupture, Murfreesboro, Tennessee, November 5, 1996*, PAB-99/03. Washington, DC: NTSB.

----. 1998. *Release of Hazardous Liquid, Grammercy, Louisiana, May 23, 1996*, PAB-98/01. Washington, DC: NTSB.

----. 1995. *Texas Eastern Transmission Corporation Natural Gas Pipeline Explosion and Fire, Edison, New Jersey March 23, 1994*, PAR-95/01. Washington, DC: NTSB.

----. 1993. *Highly Volatile Release from Underground Storage Cavern and Explosion, Mapco Natural Gas Liquids, Inc., Brenham, Texas, April 7, 1992*, PAR-93/01. Washington, DC: NTSB.

NiSource (NiSource Gas Transmission & Storage). 2012. *Control Room Management Plan*, August 1, 2011, revised October 8, 2012. Merrillville, Indiana: NiSource.

www.ingramcontent.com/pod-product-compliance
Lightning Source LLC
Chambersburg PA
CBHW080915290526
45795CB00007BA/2529